ARCHANGELOLOGY ARCHANGEL BREATH-TAP

IF YOU CALL THEM THEY WILL COME

KIM CALDWELL

Archangelology LLC

A Division of Archangelology LLC

https://archangelology.com

Introduction Editing and enhancement Rachel Caldwell

Book Editing Grammarly

ISBN: 978-1-947284-19-7

❀ Created with Vellum

1

ABOUT THE SERIES

"Logic will get you from point A to B. Imagination will take you everywhere."-- Einstein

~

This piece is one of a series of Angelic Upgrade books that fill you with Divine Angelic codes. Angelic laws are based on love and light thus, operate for free-will, so we must call and ask the Archangels for help.

When working with your book relax, take deep breaths and ground to Mother Earth. Focus on Intentions for whatever it is your heart desires that are for the highest good of all involved. Intentions for these energies that we can not see but feel when we are ready. There are those that believe The Archangels are the Ones that make Law of Attraction Work.

This series of books take on a life of its own as the Archangels move and play from book to book, creating a Delicious Alchemy. Each book becomes an instrument in this Celestial Symphony for a more fulfilling life. Many of the Archangel books also carry and infuse the Violet Flame and Divine Connection to Mother Earth for a transformational experience.

Each book has a matching meditation audio available for your listening pleasure at http://www.togetherpublishing.com. Please visit our site for your gifts. The book and the audio have similar wording, yet according to the Archangels, they Upgrade us differently. Each medium has a unique experience, energetically Upgrading us in distinct ways. Each time you read or hear an Archangel Upgrade, a new dimension is added or adjusted for your benefit.

Become interactive with your book; when inspired, read the words aloud, and let them roll over you, feeling the love and magic that the Angels radiate. When inspired create your own rituals; there is no right or wrong way. As you play with the rock stars of the Celestial realm, you can expect your life to become more heavenly, more peaceful.

You may Notice Many Words are Uniquely Capitalized throughout this series; this is yet another way the Angels infuse us. When you see this try to feel that word or phrase; sensing the depth of its Intensity of Pure Divine Light throughout your Being.

The Archangel Energy is neither male nor female. This gender fluidity is made clear in this series by the use of the word they or she/he to convey a non-gender energy that shifts roles to uplift and nurture you. The upgrades happen in Divine Time, and there is no schedule. There is no competition. There is no rush. Wherever you are in the process is perfect.

A word about the length of this book. "Less is more." This Series of books is the result of decades of study in the art of Law of

Attraction, Angelic knowing and energy heal-ing, condensed here for you in a format that will shift and benefit the reader. If you found your way here, you can expect miracles. As Einstein said, "There are only two ways to live your life. One is as though nothing is a mira-cle. The other is as though everything is a miracle." The matching audio to this book is 44 minutes, so working with that is always an option.

Both Neville Goddard and Albert Einstein stated that our imagination is the creative force. Goddard went so far as to imply that our imagination is the God/dess Energy. I mention this to you because as you read these words with much more than your eyes, let your imagination run wild with vivid pictures of the love the magical Archangels have for you and of your adventures together. Enjoy.

ABOUT ARCHANGEL BREATH-TAP

~

If you are here experiencing this time-space reality as well as reading this book, you are a pioneer. I often think that we are in the "Wild West" of energy. It is all new. Humans are becoming aware that just because we can not see a "thing" does not mean it is not real or does not exist. This also creates a challenge because we are in a time where our energy alignment is becoming more important than ever, yet there does not appear to be a "user guide" for maintaining a healthy energy body. There are emerging teachings, and like anything else, we must be discerning. So I present this book to you with this request, "take the best and leave the rest." Everyone is unique and an individual. What works for you may not work for another and vice versa — this book is just a beginning to your energy studies. One thing is for sure, the more we focus and practice having a healthy energy body, the more we will learn and benefit.

We take a lot of liberties with our language in this book. Some of these words are not practiced regularly in everyday language. We do this with the intent of creating new thought, questions, and answers to enhance our lives for the highest good. We set intentions that these words bring in refreshing energies that create more well-being in our lives. Neville Goddard and Albert Einstein both implied that imagination is a creative force, and we will build on the shoulders of giants here. Yes, again you are a pioneer of new thought, energy and so much more, what an exciting time to **Be**. This energy is very high vibrational, and a little bit goes a long way. Be sure to listen to your guidance and take breaks from this process and book when called to. Some days a sentence or nothing may be enough. Always enjoy the process — no hurries or pressure. There is a gorgeous term called "Latent Learning" and what it means is that sometimes we study a subject and don't really get it. Later we all of a sudden understand things. That will happen a lot with this process so just relax and enjoy. I love when Abraham-Hicks talks about how if a little baby falls we don't say "get up you little dummy" we have patience. Please have much patience for yourself during this journey.

The Archangels are here at this time to help us tune-up and work with our energetic bodies. The human has fluent multi-dimensional energy bodies and intuitive magical fingers, the two go *hand in hand*. This energy field invisibly surrounds our physical body, with capabilities we are only beginning to understand. One thing is clear if we ask questions more answers will come. In this book we set intentions to invigorate and heal our light bodies, also known as our energetic body with the help of the Archangels. As we set intentions, unseen beneficial forces move for us. I want to remind you that you are already working with your energetic light-body, many times unknowingly. We get more focused with more intention here. You are a Master and the Archangels are here to assist you. You are a pioneer in this Energetic Universe and will explore many dimensions and worlds **Together** with your Archangels. May this book bring you Peace and Blessings.

I have worked with energy, meditation, Emotional Freedom Technique (EFT), Archangels, and breath-work for years, they have naturally become an Alchemy of sorts. Each powerful process stands on its own, so imagine the life enhancements when combined. The results must be experienced to understand how transformative they can be. I want to add that in life people will always have challenges. This is simply another tool to help us "surf the waves" as I like to envision it. May this help you in marvelous ways.

First and foremost, may I give a huge

thank you to Gary Craig, the creator of EFT (emotional freedom technique) also known as Tapping. His work has helped the lives of so many, including mine.

I discovered Tapping (EFT), which I included in one of my first books *Activate Your Abundance*, through going to a natural doctor. I went to get help with an issue; I am a big fan of reaching out for help when we need it. I went to this practitioner and paid them 80 dollars an hour to tap on me while we discussed things I wanted to improve. I would walk out of this person's office feeling relieved and happier. Working with this natural doctor went on for a few years during which time I discovered a book on an exciting subject called Emotional Freedom Technique (EFT) or Tapping. Imagine my delight when I discovered that I could tap on myself and make positive changes.

The more we can take everyone else out of the equation and stop all blame with the knowing that we can Focus and call our Archangels to help fix things, the better our life will get.

We have tools to assist us with being

Whole at the very tip of our fingers. Help from humans is lovely, yet if we get conscious that the **Divine** Archangels offer us support on a **Whole** new level, this gives us unique opportunities. If we can stop and ask for help, we may Activate unseen beneficial energies that can help us in ways we only imagined. This again is where calling your Archangels will come into this process.

Calling these Archangels works; magic works every time, the trick is to become super patient and release any preconceived timelines. Let the magic happen in its own time and way and relax. "Ask, and it is given" as Abraham-Hicks reminds us.

I want to clarify that anything we discuss in this book is intended to enhance your choice of a health care practitioner. This book is not to be used instead of health care, but rather, it is a potent bonus.

Ancient knowledge is not always taught in the mainstream; I bring this to you with the help of the Archangels. The Archangels have come to us at this time because they want to teach us more about our energetic bodies; they want to improve our lives. One thing that we must understand is that we have to ask for help. Our Universe operates on free will, and the Archangels will not intervene unless asked. Today we embark on yet another journey in learning how to ask these magnificent, magical beings to help us while assisting them in the process. The Archangels are calling for a more interactive experience. As we get conscious of our thoughts, take deep healing breaths, and tap with intention; things will begin to shift for the better. Know in your heart that you have found a gift that works. Have faith and play with this process. We can step into our power, and it just *"Tappens"* naturally, pun intended. We take deep breaths; we tap on the body's energy system, and our light body benefits.

The conscious human is bombarded with so many thoughts and frequencies at different times; they simply cannot all be our own. It is up to us to STOP and question these negative thoughts. Are they ours? I think not. As humans become more telepathic and able to feel and hear others thoughts, this is a gift, yet it can create challenges. At times humans send negative energy; it is just how we cope with stress, so no shame or blame lets just clear it. Also, be aware, there are beings that feed on negative emotions and do not have our best interest at heart; some call them entities or attachments, just to name a few. Their names are not important, becoming aware and calling for help from the Archangels is the **Focus** here. How do we stop thoughts that do not serve us and create anxiety and stress? The Archangels can help us to help ourselves with all of this. We get very conscious, and we call for **Divine** help as we tap to align the bodies energy field while taking slow deep breaths.

There are also some Intentional Switchwords in this piece. Switchwords were created by James Mangan and may be explored further in my book *Activate Your Abundance*. Switcwords turn **On** the Subconscious mind like a light. Picture flipping the light switch **On**. Here are the ones included. **Together** is the Master Switchword which brings **Together** the conscious, subconscious, and superconscious mind to become all we can **BE**. **Whole** means to be **Whole**, healed and happy. **Up** means to lift our Vibration to a better place. **Be** means to **Be** Well, **Whole** and happy. **Divine** creates miracles or the extraordinary. **Love** puts a healing balm on anything it touches. **Reach** is to find something that is lost. **Focus** to direct Divine Intelligence. **Now** is to come into this moment fully in our power for the highest good. **On** is to bring in **Divine** Mind. Allow these words to spark your imagination and power when you encounter them. I want to add that I have worked with James Mangan who is non-physical for so long now that I may have intermingled some new Switchwords in the mix. This is to remind you that you may create your own Switchwords and turn your subconscious **On** anytime you desire. You are that connected and tuned in. Remember as Florence Shinn said "Your Word Is Your Wand.

You will notice that we use the word **Now** a lot in this book. Anytime you see the word now take this as an opportunity to get in the now moment where all your power is. Most of us have heard of the "*Power Of Now*" from the great Echart Tolle. This is a chance to use this wisdom to our advantage. When you see the word **Now** picture your life happy and glowing and your Breath-Tap working its magic for you.

This is a powerful process that may create shifts. Of course, we set intentions that this happens with Grace and Ease. If you find yourself needing to take breaks, please do so. Drink plenty of good clean water and take hot sea salt baths to integrate the process. Be patient and easy on yourself.

Spending time with Archangels creates a heavenly life. The information I have put together is meant to work for your individualized wants and needs. It is not a prescribed set of general steps or rules, but rather it aims to help you in your particular journey and give you what you need to begin or grow in a mindset. There is no right or wrong way to use this tool. The only thing I recommend you keep in the forefront of your practice is to ensure you are enjoying the process. The Archangelology Book and Audio Series is here to help you at this time. If you call the Archangels they will come. For gifts from the Archangels visit http://www. togetherpublishing.com.

Now, let's get started.

3

ARCHANGEL BREATH-TAP

∼

During one of the darkest periods of my life, I was blessed to find and learn to call on the Archangels; this discovery brought about the Archangelology book and audio Series. For the last decade, I have brought meditation audios with great joy. In each of these audios, I have asked everyone to take deep, healing breaths. Deep, healing breath-work has been practiced for eons, as far back as anyone can even imagine. Breath is life. Breath is the prana. Breath is the primordial, deep, taking in of the God/dess Source. Take a deep, healing breath with me now. For eons, people pressed or tapped upon their body in different ways to evoke positive reactions. Many call this acupressure. Then an amazing man came along Gary Craig and brought us EFT. Emotional Freedom Technique or tapping on the body.

Today, I present to you the knowledge that if we combine these proven, productive processes. **Together**, this will create Alchemy where the benefits are exponential. There are too many benefits from each of these processes, each school of thought to mention. As we pull these **Divine** gifts, **Together**, we are in for a life-enhancing, and evolving process that it is my intention will bless the rest of your life. We are setting intentions with the help of the Archangels to invigorate and heal our light body, also known as our energetic body. This energy field that surrounds our body is the Focus of our **Up**liftment in this book. As we set intentions, unseen forces move to support us.

. . .

If you dedicate a daily practice of deep breathing with your Archangels and tapping, you can expect to create more well-being. These practices are also a great help during any challenges, so knowing them is to your advantage. As they say, "practice makes perfect." I also feel that these magical practices are aligned with feeling better. Gently tap your thymus (the middle of your chest) as you say to yourself or aloud, "I am attracting things to make me happy, vibrant, and healthy while taking deep, slow breaths. As rich, clean oxygen feeds your mind, body, and spirit.

You may boost your Breath-Tap by practicing when connected to Mother Earth. When inspired experiment with practicing your Breath-Tap outdoors with bare feet on the earth. Mother Earth pulls vast volumes of dense energy out of our energetic field and balances us. The electromagnetic fields of Mother Earth attune us and raise our Vibration **Up**. Even 5 minutes a day grounded and connected to the earth will infuse your energy body with more Peace, **Love**, and light. If you do not have access to a comfy place to practice on mother earth now, use your imagination.

As we start upon this journey, and I want to let you know that it is a journey because when we go on a journey, things evolve, things change. We don't expect anything to stay in a static way. While you're taking this journey, know that you will evolve this process intuitively. Our Angelic Breath-Tap is an affirming living process that will enhance you. You will flavor your Angelic Breath-Tap with your unique style, gifts, ideas, and this will make it even stronger for you. Understand that Angelic Breath-Tap is something that you can take with you throughout your entire life. You can always have this blessed practice and sacred ability to create more of the life you want. EFT is a fantastic gift. As we tap upon different areas of the body, while holding intentions and specific thoughts, this allows us to calm the system and help the energy flow. Imagine when a kettle is boiling and whistling, and we open the lid to let off some steam. To cool things down in the body, we tap to release stress and tension. While we're doing this, we can **Focus**. **Focus** is one of our most essential tools. It's one of the most valuable skills to develop, combined with our imagination. As we learn to **Focus**, turn our mind in the direction we desire, and add our Breath-Tap, we are creating on dimensions that are new and exciting to humans.

We're living in a vast sea of distractions. There's no other way to put it. We have so many things going on that take our attention away from what it is we want, and sometimes the trickiest thing is to quiet our mind. As we learn to get centered and **Focus** on what we desire for longer periods, we will find that life flows in a more swimmingly and enchanting way. Take deep healing breaths and tap your chest gently as you say, "Archangel Raziel, please give me the wisdom and concentration to **Focus** on things that will make me happy, healthy and abundant or something better." Tap, breathe and feel the Archangels help and love for you. Spend as long as feels good doing this now.

Once again, if we bring our **Focus on** what we desire and we play with the breath, and the tapping, we're going to start to uncover our innate ability to create kingdoms, to create mighty, exciting adventures that we only dreamed. As you're reading this book, please continue to take deep, slow breaths. **Focus** is how our breath work is going to enhance and bless us. We're going to work with the most straightforward process possible. You're going to breathe all the way in through your nose. The goal is to pull the breath deep in the lungs, filling the diaphragm. Then you're going to exhale through your nose gently. Add pressing your tongue to the roof of your mouth, while closing your lips and exhaling out through your nose and you are activating an acupressure point. Try that with me now. Call Archangel Metatron, the Archangel of Sacred Geometry and Well-Being to stand by you and take a deep, healing breath. Now release that breath through your nose. Yes, and feel the power while you're pressing your tongue up against the roof of your mouth. Feel the seal. Feel how this seal creates calm energy in the body. Yes. If inspired, ask Archangel Metatron to adjust your energy or chi for the highest good while you do this and tap your chest or any place that feels right in the moment. That is perfect. Feel the relaxation and flow. See your energy running correctly in your mind's eye. See a stream of sparkling golden energy moving throughout your body along your energy channels. Let your imagination and intuition do this. It is common for individuals to express they do not know how to work with their imagination. Let me be clear that you are a master with the Archangels help. If you are calling on and trying to work with your imagination, significant benefits are happening. Know that when you activate your imagination, you are becoming more skilled with it each time. Tap with me and say. "Archangel Gabriel, please stand with me to give me Hope and Faith that every time I work with my imagination, I get better at it. Please help me to create wonderful blessings with my imagination. Guide me in using my creative energy for the highest good of all involved. Thank you, Archangel Gabriel." Have confidence and faith. Your Archangels are guiding you, and you're making progress.

One of the most productive things we may **Focus** on is our blessings and how grateful we are for all that we have. The Moon Angels are very effective at helping us raise our mood. So they will be assisting us in this with the help of Archangel Sandalphon, the Archangel of Music who takes our prayers to the God/dess Source. Take a deep, healing breath and tap the side of your thumb together with your pointer finger. We are going to get a little beat going. Sing with me now, "Archangel Sandalphon and Moon Angels, please surround me with your **Uplifting Melodic** energies as I tap on all that I am grateful for. I want to first and foremost thank the Source God/dess energy for my gifts; I know that sometimes I ask for things and forget to express my gratitude please let me sing it to you now. Let Archangel Sandalphon take all my gratitude to you so that you understand that all you do for me is appreciated. I am thankful for the eyes to see this. I am grateful for the lungs to take deep breaths and fill me with your **Divine** Energy. Thank you for my hands to hold all that life is gifting me. Thank you to my feet that pivot and move forward in life. Thank you. Thank you. Thank you gorgeous Archangels for all you do for me. Thank you, **Divine** Energies for blessing me with the mind to integrate all this **Love** into my light body, to feel my freedom and joy. I am grateful for the beautiful earth and all her gifts she bestows on me." Take a deep healing breath and smile as you tap. See the gorgeous Goddess Gaia; mother earth stand before you as well. Feel as all these **Divine** Beings surround you and hear a melodic choir of Angels singing as these beautiful energies infuse you. Feel the Moon Angels beautiful luminescent silver light moving through your energetic body tingling you as Archangel Sandalphon gently brushes their Angel Wings up and down your energetic body. Feel the magnificent tingles and pulses of Light, as your energy body aligns, and freedom rocks your soul on this melodic journey. **Divine** Angelic Wings brush anything out of your energy field that is not for your highest good. Feel as Mother Earth sends deep magnetic pulses of energy to you. **Now**, anchor deep into this moment and feel all the **Love** and support around you. Feel how safe and adored you are.

Reach is a favorite Switchword of mine. **Reach** is to find something that is lost. I present the idea of using **Reach** to align with, blissful, peaceful emotional states **Together**. Take a deep healing breath and tap, remembering how loved and supported you are. You may want to do this while playing some delightful music by Mozart, Tchaikovsky, or anyone you **Love**. Get in a grove with your Breath-Tap and appreciation. Make a game of it and play it often. You may do this anywhere and anytime. Yes, Breath-Tap **Love** and gratitude right into your body and set intentions for the Archangels and Mother

Earth to infuse your energetic body with well-being and appreciation. Feel your spirits rising **Up** as you Breath-Tap on how blessed and fortunate you are. Let the Silver Shimmering Moon Angel Light permeate your energy field and dissolve anything that is clogging or holding you back. Let the Angelic tones vibrate out any discordant energy blocks or patches. Take your time and feel the freedom. Feel Archangel light wings touch and support you, as you float and shimmer in this **Divine** Sacred Healing Energy Bath. The Mozart effect is the understanding that music can positively affect our mind, and I would like to add the possibility that music can positively enhance our energetic body as well. Archangel Sandalphon wants to remind you to **Reach** for your music to improve your mood and feel **Uplifted**. The Moon Angels wish to remind you that when you feel down, this is alright, feel these feelings while calling for help from your **Divine** Archangels. If you call them, they will come to assist and lift you **Up**.

. . .

Now, I'm going to include for you at the back of this book a lovely chart that shows you different tapping points you may explore. This chart was from my second book almost a decade ago called *Activate Your Abundance*. Tapping has stood the test of time and become even more prevalent **now**. You have found something that is going to help when you play with it. You may have other areas on your body that you would like to experiment tapping on. It's a simple process, and as you tap on different areas of your body, you are enlivening your energetic body, some people call this chi. You're helping this energetic body to enliven and tune the physical body. Your creating a Vortex for this energy to flow freely in a productive manner. Tapping with the long slow breaths is such a **Divine**ly intelligent process. As you use Breath-Tap with Focus and intention, you will help the bodies **Divine** Intelligence to Activate on all Dimensions of time and space, calling in Higher Aspects of Yourself. As you develop this process expect exponential results. It is exciting to practice visualizing the energy flowing with **Love** and light through the body. You may see this energy flow as sparkles of the Violet Flame that we work with so often in the Archangelology Series. You may feel another color; ultimately, you will intuit which colors feel best, and this may change from time to time. There are no rules except to enjoy the process, get creative with your Archangels.

Let's say, for instance, there is a discomfort in the body. One can take deep, slow healing breaths, and tap gently on a specific area or around an uncomfortable zone. Do a setup phrase that goes something like this. "Even though I am experiencing this discomfort in the body, I still deeply **Love** and accept myself." One may tap on the areas that I have put in the chart, or they may tap gently on the chest area. Another excellent area to gently tap on is the sacral chakra, the area around the belly button. This is a powerful energy center and it is great to gently stimulate the energy flow here.

. . .

As you're breathing deep, taking in all that sweet oxygen to calm the mind and body. You're tapping gently on or around the area that you want to send lots of **Love** to, and you're saying to your mind, body, spirit and energetic body, "I deeply **Love** and accept myself." Take a deep, healing breath as you visualize relaxation flowing through your being and feel Archangel Metatron standing beside and supporting you. This **Divine** technique is going to shift many things in powerful ways. With practice, this puts us back in the driver seat of observing our thoughts and directing them for our highest good. The **Divine** Catherine Ponder coined a term called "Chemicalization." Catherine explained that sometimes before life feels better, it might feel a little hard. Be aware this can happen and know you're on the right track. When this happens, it is time to give ourselves more **Love** and support. Be easy on yourself. Do things that provide you with pleasure, take hot sea salt baths, drink plenty of clean water, enjoy time outdoors, or any activity that relaxes you. "This too, shall pass."

Now, the understanding with tapping, breath-work, and Archangels, is to be very patient and give them time to go in and do their **Divine** Magic. This information is to go with any doctor or professional healer a person is working with, and boost it. Now, if someone is trying to find a professional care-giver, they can also do the tapping to help relax, and find an excellent match to help with their situation. When I said that, let's take a deep, healing breath. I work with amazing healers who support me. The Course of Miracles has a lovely saying, "we are not healed alone." To me, this says it is not only alright to accept help; it is **Divine.** Let us release any mindset that implies it is weak to need help. We are human, we all need help from time to time, and it is intelligent to seek it. "Seek, and you will find and the other famous saying "Ask and it is given" is the title to an Abraham-Hicks book.

A favorite place to tap on the body that you can do anytime, anywhere is right on your breast bone where your heart is. As we remember to think with our heart and become heart-centered, we find life flowing in more loving, happy ways. Call on Archangel Haniel, the Archangel of **Love** now and ask them to help us be more heart-centered and make decisions with our heart more. You may take a deep, healing breath, and you may tap. And you may say any phrase to yourself that you want to tap into the body, mind, and spirit. You may say, "I am creating the **Divine** life I desire with my heart. I am radiating **Divine Love**. I am **Whole**, I am happy, I am healed." Deep, healing breath. While you're tapping and you're taking these slow, deep healing breaths intending to bring the, I Am energy into the body with the help of Archangel Haniel. Feel Archangel Haniel standing beside you, supporting you, loving you. Feel how supported and **Love**d you are. An excellent place to tap is the bottom of your feet. There are numerous acupressure points there to explore. Get creative, let your Archangels guide your fingers. Any place on your body that calls you and feels good is great to tap now.

· · ·

The I AM phrase has been practiced for eons. It was known to be used by the Miracle Maker Moses. As you tap phrases into your body on your chest, around the heart area, let's pull in a little Archangel magic. Take a deep, healing breath slowly, and call to your left side, "Archangel Michael, please stand on my left to protect me and to guide me while I do this tapping." Deep, healing breath. Archangel Raziel, please stand to my right to bring me Wisdom while I'm tapping, to show me the best way and the best places to tap on my body." Another deep, healing breath. "Archangel Uriel, please stand behind me to bring me Peace and Protection as I tap on my body. Yes, thank you, Archangel Uriel." Take another deep, healing breath. And before you, please call Archangel Zadkiel. Archangel Zadkiel is one of the keepers of the Violet Flame and the Archangel of Forgiveness. So we ask that Archangel Zadkiel stands in front of us, as we are gently tapping on our chest, on our heart area, while we're connecting to the beautiful

Mother Earth and pulling in all this heart-centered energy. **Now** say, "Archangel Zadkiel run your Violet Flame through all space, time, and dimensions of my lives. I ask that the Violet Flame come in and run through every cell of my mind, body, and spirit." I ask that Zadkiel run the Violet Flame, and clear and heal all my mitochondria and DNA. Bless my cells with **Divine** Light, **Love**, Peace, and Happiness. I am blessed with joy, Bliss, and I see the Violet Flame running all around me and through every cell in my energetic bodies." I see my hands ignited with the Violet Flame, and I see the Violet Flame surrounding me, wrapping around me, soothing me, healing me, expanding me, giving me more **Divine** Thought, giving me Forgiveness of myself and Forgiveness of everyone around me." Take a deep, healing breath. And now we tap again. Take deep healing breaths, and tap. Working with the thymus heart area and our Archangels are going to bring great soulful **Love** and Light. May this happen for the highest of all with Grace and Ease.

. . .

As we're doing this, we're helping the energy, the chi to run throughout our body. And as it runs throughout our body and circulates, we see the beautiful Violet Flame clearing, cleaning, healing all our blood, energy, life force. Yes. Take a deep, refreshing breath and tap.

Another favorite place I like to tap that people don't necessarily know I'm tapping **On** for privacy is right at the top of my knee. This privacy tapping works when I am sitting with my legs under a table. Take a deep, fortifying breath as you tap on your knee, and ask Archangel Jophiel to come in and stand to your left. **Now** ask that Archangel Jophiel, help release all judgment from your mind, body, spirit, from your energetic bodies. We ask that Jophiel help us to see things with non-judgmental eyes, as we stop judging others, we can stop judging ourself for more Peace.

Taking full responsibility for anything that is

going **On** in our lives puts us entirely in our power. **Now** Breath-Tap and say "I ask that Archangel Orion come into my energy field and help release all blame I have toward another. Archangel Gabriel, please come in and give me hope and faith that as I release anyone else, my life will move to a happier place that brings me Peace." Let's tap on the top of our head to set intentions for higher conscious to flow. Releasing judgment and taking responsibility is going to help on incredible levels, be easy on yourself. Unproductive emotions also include guilt, Ask the Archangels to help release all guilt and self-loathing from your energetic bodies while using your Breath-Tap **Now**. This process takes time and patience and the help of the Archangels.

Now, our knee area is fascinating because when people are having discomfort with their knees, there could be some energy stuck and a fear of moving forward in life. Everyone goes through a fear of moving forward in life at times. This is part of being human. It's nothing to judge or to feel uncomfortable about. We're going to do some statements in a moment to clear on that.

To our other side, we're going to ask that Archangel Gabriel, the Archangel of Hope stand with us. It is so beautiful how Archangel Gabriel can come in and give us Hope. Hope and understanding that if we have Hope, everything's going to **Be** alright. Imagination and Breath-Tap, are so powerful, and we are creating blessings through all time, space, and dimensions. As Neville Goddard said, "Imagination is the preview to life's coming attractions." We want to **Focus** our imagination for a marvelous **Now** and future. If one believes and sets intentions, we may set up blessings for future lives. This is up to you and your beliefs, if you would like to do so set intentions **Now** for a glorious sparkling future where your free, happy, healthy, and abundantly blessed.

We have the gorgeous Archangel Gabriel on

one side and the gorgeous Archangel Jophiel on the other, and we're going to tap on our knees. Now ask that Archangel Raziel stand before you and guide you to give you the Wisdom to know which way to go and how to move forward for the highest good. And we're going to say this statement as we Breath-Tap, "Even though I have some fears about moving forward in my life, I still deeply **Love** and accept myself. I know that **Divine** Forces are guiding me now," Continue your Breath-Tap. Breathe deep and slow. Feel how protected and guided you are by your Archangels. Let all the stress leave your body. Take another deep, healing breath. And say, "Even though I have some fears and some stress about moving forward in my life, I still deeply **Love** and accept myself. I know everything will be alright and actually is alright now." Deep, healing breath. Tap gently. Tap with intention. Tap to know that everything is in **Divine** Order, that we are being guided, that the God/dess energy has your back, that the Archangels have your back. Deep, healing breath as you continue to tap. Breath-Tap to remember your safe now. Feel how safe and calm you are.

You can do this anytime, anywhere. You can have your legs under a table and tap, and no one will even know you're working on you.

If a trigger occurs, as we all have triggers because we've all had unwanted experiences in our lives. Again, seek professional help when you need it. While in the meantime doing your tapping because tapping and deep breath-work are powerful self-help tools to remove stress from the energetic bodies. When we have a thought that plays over, that has been triggered by something; we can call in Archangel Zadkiel to run the Violet Flame while we're tapping and taking deep, slow breaths. See the Violet Flame infusing us and bringing us Peace and Light.

Now, another easy place to tap is your thumb with the side of your pointer finger **Together**.

You can put your hand in a discreet place and call Archangel Camael, who is the Archangel of Courage. Camael is a master at helping us handle stress. You can take deep, slow, focused breaths, and say, "Even though I have experienced stress in the past, I still deeply love and accept myself and I feel this stress leaving now." Pull another deep, healing breath, as you tap. Again we say, "Even though I have experienced stress or anxiety, I still deeply love and accept myself, and let it all go now." Deep, healing breaths while tapping. Now, feel the energy flowing through your body more freely. Feel the breath pumping slowly, gently, clearing, improving your emotions. Know that Archangel Camael has your back and best interests. **Focus**ing on good emotions will help you in all areas of your life, and Camael is here to Support and **Love** you in this now.

Did you ever consider that you can guide energy healing with the help of the Archangels? Did you ever consider that you were given every single tool that you could possibly need? I'm setting intentions that the Archangels help only the best and perfect information get through to you and that you will take, only what is for your highest good.

Take a deep, healing breath. Now, another beautiful thing that the Breath-Tap does is it raises **Up** the vibration. We are all vibrational beings. As we raise our vibrations **Up**, we start to feel better. As we Breath-Tap intending to raise our vibration, and we take deep, healing breaths, we begin to feel our energy align. We start to lift. We start to feel our energy soar, and then we take a deep, healing breath. We do the tapping in the perfect place. Say with me now, "I call in Archangel Orion to help me see the perfect places to tap on my body, on my vessel while I'm taking sweet, deep breaths. To bring more **Love** into my life, to bring more Light into my life, to make me enjoy life more easily, to remind me to count my blessings and feel how blessed I am. Archangel Orion, please stand by my side and help while I'm tapping." You may want to tap on your hips right at the hip joint to help move forward in life with more ease. You may want to tap on the heart area. Tap on the heart area to open the heart to more **Love**, to more Light, to more freedom. Tap on the forehead and say the powerful creative statement, "I crown my life with Success **Now**."

Take a deep, healing breath. Archangel Orion stands with us. So strong, so supportive, so patient. Like a parent would stand with their child, patiently showing them the way, leading them. Tap slowly and let the body release anything that no longer serves. Yes. That's it. Archangel Orion, thank you. Take a deep, healing breath.

Now you may also try tapping on your third eye area, that is on your forehead between your eyebrows, and say, "I'm guided. I feel the perfect way to proceed." And call in Archangel Raziel, the Archangel of Wisdom and Magic. Ask Archangel Raziel to show you the way to go to experience more **Love**

and magic in your life. Deep, healing breath as you tap your brow area.

Now, as you're tapping your body and you feel the beautiful Archangel Orion and Archangel Raziel around you, we're going to create some Archangel Alchemy. Archangel Sandalphon is the Archangel of Harmony and Music, please call them in now to help with this melodic infusion. Feel as these Radiant Archangels are facing you, and they put their hands **Together**, creating a sparkling circle of light around you as melodic Angelic tones fill the air. While the atmosphere lifts, please tap on the area of your body that feels like it needs a little extra **Love**. And take deep, healing, slow breaths. Now, feel as Archangel Orion, Archangel Sandalphon, Archangel Haniel, Archangel Raziel and the Moon Angels, move around you, infusing your energetic body to clear it and remove anything that is not for your highest good. See Archangel Metatron enter with their golden light net to remove anything that is not for your highest good.

They move this net all around and through your energy field as long as is needed to freshen you. This is all done with Grace and Ease.

Angels help after you've asked them because Archangels must be asked. Sing now, "Archangel Haniel, Archangel Sandalphon, and Archangel Orion, please stand with me and remove any parasitic beings or entities that are not for my highest good with grace and ease. Gently dissolving them and sending them back to the light." Relax and take deep, slow breaths and tap and sing, "Even though I get depressed or sad sometimes, I still deeply love and accept myself." Deep, healing breath. Let's do it again. "Even though I get sad or depression, sometimes, I still deeply love and accept myself." Now Breath-Tap. "Archangels, please help bring in more **Love**, higher consciousness, more cosmic consciousness. Download me now with your higher **Love**." I can hear that song going in the background, "Bring me a higher **Love**." As the music surrounds us, as we're infused with **Love**, Light, Angel magic, and Angel Alchemy. Feel this magical melodic experience filling your being through all space, time, and dimension, bringing the delicious Angelic healing and Light Codes into your energetic field on all timelines.

Tap on the belly button area with deep breaths. Feel Archangel Orion, Archangel Sandalphon and Archangel Haniel pull out any heavy, traumatic energy or experiences that are not for your highest good, and know that they will continue working on you for hours, days, even weeks after you do this process. At a very gentle, slow pace where you barely even realize it's happening. One day, maybe in a month or a year, you'll think, "Wow. I feel great." And then all of a sudden you'll remember, "Oh yes, the Archangels have my back, all I have to do is ask them for help. Oh yes, I called the Archangels in, and I asked them to help me with this issue that the collective consciousness deals with now, the issue of depression, of anxiety, these issues that happen." Please understand that many times, these depressing thoughts are not our own and could be entity attachments or the feelings we pick up from others and ask the Archangels for help with this. They want you to know this is their **Divine** Pleasure to help us now. They are here to help us now. Always remember this. The Archangels want to help us learn to work with and heal our energetic bodies. This is a new process for many, and as we work with the Archangels, we will get more guidance and ideas on how to enhance our energetic body. This is just a tiny beginning. If inspired, you will take this work much further and make much greater strides. May this book **Be** the beginning of wonderful health, happiness, abundance, and blessings for you and yours. Get creative and juicy with your Archangels and Breath-Tap. The Archangels love to help and play with you. When you hear loving, helpful advice and ideas that feel great to you, this is your Archangels speaking with you. The more you work with them, the easier it gets to hear them and trust that what you are hearing is real. You are a magical Angelic connector for the planet earth. Bless you. Feel your Magnetic Angel Wings flutter at your back. Yes, you have Angel Wings and to Activate them simply picture them in your mind's eye. They connect you to the Angelic Realms and help you hear and make contact with your Archangels.

I want to say something now that is very important that I learned from a Divine Energy Healer, Christopher Macklin. If a person ever has really scary thoughts of wanting to leave earth, seek professional help, and reach out, ask for help. And please be aware there could be negative, entity attachments on that person pushing these thoughts on them. My point in telling you this is, it is possible these thoughts might not be their own. I found a lot of help from Christopher Macklin for removing unwanted entities. I listed his book in the back-references. He does offer group healing on a donation basis so that anyone can afford to get help. Everyone is different so keep seeking help, and you will find it. Yes. Call in the Archangels to protect your energy, to stand by you. Call in Archangel Michael to stand before you, to stand by you, to stand behind you to keep any disruptive energies away. If we call these Archangels, they will come in and help us. Now, we do our part too. Of course, we reach out for help from professionals. We talk. We reach out, and we ask for the help we need. And we take deep, slow, healing breaths while we're tapping on the body to help the body let off that stress, calm down, and come back into a better place. And we flow our breath; we continue to breathe.

We bring in the powerful imagination now because as the great Einstein said, "Imagination can take us anywhere," and we visualize ourselves in our safest, warmest, happiest place while we tap the body. I am seeing myself wrapped in a loving Archangels Wings just floating, smiling peacefully and so relaxed. You may choose this vision or create your own. We keep doing this until our emotions move to a softer, better place so we can relax. We focus on soothing emotions.

Take a deep, healing breath. You have it. You are that powerful. You are a magnificent being of light. Humans are becoming more and more telepathic **now**. What this means is many times when we're having thoughts that feel uncomfortable; they are not our thoughts. **Be** very aware that this can happen and take your deep, healing breaths and stop and center yourself and call your Archangels, do this regularly throughout the day. You may want to set a timer around your home or on your phone that reminds you twice a day to do your Breath-Tap and call on your Archangels for back up and support.

Now, once you are ready, excellent, let's tap on our body and do some of the I Am powerful statements. Let's Breath-Tap on what we want. Abraham-Hicks has a term that they call "segment intending." This is such a beautiful practice, and it is akin to what I do with calling Angels before I walk into a building. You intend that great things will happen throughout the day instead of just letting the day happen. Call in your

Angels, and you ask them to help you create a gorgeous, beautiful day. Now take a deep, healing breath.

For instance, every morning, when we wake up, we might spend three minutes doing our Breath-Tap as we say, "Archangel Gabriel the Archangel of Hope and Raphael the Archangel of Health and Abundance, please stand with me as I am experiencing a fantastic day. I am rendezvousing with the people I love. I am having fun. I am finding fun things to do. I am enjoying my own company. I am loving being with myself and having fun with friends. I am loving exploring. I am smiling, and I am laughing because it feels so good." You might want to smile as you tap and say, "I am finding things today that make me laugh. I am, I am, I am." You will pick what you **Love**, and you will program this into your subconscious with your Breath-Tap and your Archangels. Does this mean that humans are like computers? Yes, this is highly possible. Does this mean that we can program ourselves to experience the life we want to? Yes, this is highly possible. And I present to you now that this is an excellent way to create more of the life you want.

You may also tap on fear, try standing in a cold shower because cold showers are super powerful for turning on chemicals in the brain that get rid of anxiety and fear. Another great place to tap gently is on your back, right where the kidneys are. The kidneys in some traditions are known to be the area that holds fear. Take a deep, healing breath while we are discussing this. The kidney area is at the top of your buttocks, near the low back on both sides. You can put both hands back there and gently tap while taking deep, healing breaths. As you tap, say, "Archangel Uriel, please help me to release any fear from my energetic body and have great Peace." Relax and smile as you're creating excellent energy flow. Take deep, healing, slow breaths. Breath-Tap is a beautiful way to gently move the energy through your body while setting intentions for how you want to feel emotionally. And if you experience any fear, tapping with your deep, slow breaths is a wonderful way to pull yourself back and then to activate your powerful imagination, to take yourself to your happy place. Try this tapping process in a cold shower for just 30 seconds to a minute if you want to chase off anxiety to create a space for good emotions. I have had great success with quick cold showers alleviating anxiety for years. It is a bit of a challenge to get started, yet well worth the effort once the magic starts happening of a lighter mind and mood.

Take a deep, healing breath. Focus very intently while you are tapping in your words. **Be** focused and intent when you are releasing things from your light body. You may want to tap, breathe and add the statement, "Even though I'm having these heavy thoughts, I still deeply love and accept myself." Once a shift happens, and you start feeling lighter, start saying, again, the things that you want. Speak your words for the blessings you wish and take your slow, deep breaths. Tap, and pull in your powerful imagination to see your Archangels all around you, see your Archangels helping you raise **Up** this **Divine** energy. Singing to and with your Archangels is powerful. Be sure to call in Archangel Sandalphon to help you expand your melodic experiences. When we Sing to our Archangels, they feel us and respond. If you would like to learn more about Archangel Sandalphon, the Archangel of harmony, they have their book and audio for you, just like all the Archangels we have discussed do. Each one is waiting to go on marvelous adventures with you for your pleasure and enjoyment.

Let us now pull in some Divine Dolphin energy. Take a deep, healing breath. I was blessed to study the work and books of Amorah Quan Yin. She was a master here on the earth, helping the **Divine** Feminine Energy to integrate lovingly and peacefully. She taught so many amazing, powerful techniques, and she Downloads us from other dimensions if we call on her. She integrates the Dolphin Energy. **Now** take a deep, healing breath, call your Archangels. Call Archangel Camael to stand on your left. Archangel Camael is the Archangel of Courage. Whenever you would like a little sparkle of courage to feel better, to let fears leave your mind, please call Archangel Camael to stand on your left and help with this. And on the other side, let's call Archangel Raphael. Raphael is the magnificent Archangel of Health and Abundance. Archangel Raphael and Archangel Camael are going to stand with us while we are tapping and taking deep, slow breaths. Breath-Tap will soothe our mind, body, and spirit, as our Dolphins come in and swirl around us. We are creating Exquisite Archangel Alchemy with the beautiful Archangel Camael's golden glowing Light Codes, and Archangel Raphael's green Light Codes. All these beautiful Light Codes and Blissful Dolphin energy are swirling around you. **Now**, as you feel these swirls of Light Codes and Dolphin Energy flowing around take a deep, healing breath and tap on your solar plexus. This is the area right above our belly button. Feel blissful Dolphins swimming all around, through your energetic body, as the Dolphins bring so many rays of color. They're bringing the white diamond light, the beautiful Golden Sun Energy, the Violet Flame, the soothing blue light, and invigorating red light. Feel these Light Codes vibrating through your energy field and making you smile, lifting your spirit. **Now** we feel the Sun Angels coming in and Breath-Tap. The beautiful Sun Angels are circling all around us, bringing the magnificent Sun Power and Archangel Raphael and Archangel Camael blend with this. Feel these radiating **Divine** light codes that are filled with all the beautiful colors, and our Dolphins are all around us. Feel the sparkles of Bliss as you hear the Dolphins singing their beautiful songs while Angelic harmony fills the air. Relax every cell in your energetic body as **Divine** Light Codes infuse your energetic body.

Now, one of the things that Amorah Quan Yin spoke of was that we each have a

Personal Dolphin Guide. Call in your Dolphin guide at this moment. Yes, feel how you want to smile. Feel how the Dolphin moves through your energetic field. They're real. You may want to ask your Dolphin their name and start communicating with them. Ask them to infuse their **Divine** Dolphin Essence in one of your crystals. This way, you may carry them with you and be reminded of them more often. You may add your Archangels essence to your crystals. This is Archangel Alchemy at its best as your imagination creates. Feel as this Dolphin break through any barriers, fear, anger, hurt, a frustration that is clogging the energetic body. Get your imagination going because imagination is that powerful. Hear the beautiful, Dolphins Singing with Archangel Sandalphon. Hear their harmonious Dolphin Angel Music they make as they're moving through your energetic body, breaking **Up** anything that is not for your highest good. Feel the joy rising **Up** through your base chakra, **Up** through all of your energy body. Feel the joy rising **Up** out of your head, and then sprinkling out all over you, lifting your spirit. Smile and feel that deep **Divine** Bliss that the Dolphins bring.

Take a deep, healing breath and tap. Feel as these Dolphins move behind you. Feel Archangel Jophiel behind you as well. Singing Angelic Dolphin **Love** Songs. Now at your belly button, see the infinity sign. See many infinity signs, moving in a circle creating a flower with your belly button at the center. See it spinning gently. See all the fear in your base chakra disappearing. Feel your power expanding in your sacral chakra, remember that you are a God/dess and powerful as the radiant Archangels and Dolphins swim all around you, yes.

Now, in front of you, we have a guest appearance and a surprise from the beautiful Saint Martha. Take a deep, healing breath. Continue to tap around your belly button. Saint Martha is a blessed saint who will come in and help create healthy boundaries in your life. Visualize the beautiful Saint

Martha standing before you, completing the circle. Feel your Sun Angels all around you. Camael, the Archangel of Courage and all these Archangels, are around you infusing you with Light Codes, with **Love**. Raphael stands beside you. They all face you infusing you; feel that you are a being of light. You are a light manifestor.

Now, gently tap and take slow breaths. Tap this into your body that you have Celestial Beings around you, guiding you, protecting you. These beings have your back. Deep, healing breath, feel the Dolphins giggling. Dolphins have a giggle. It's a beautiful, clicking sound that breaks through any barriers, that helps you move forward, that helps you to release pain and fear and raise your vibration. When a person feels sad, this is the perfect time to ask their Dolphin Guide to use their energetic clicking sounds to help break this **Up**. Of course, a person has to feel their feelings and make Peace with where they are. Then call for Celestial help.

. . .

We are powerfully activating our imaginations now. Please call in Archangel Jophiel and the magnificent Moon Angels now to help you stop judging yourself concerning using your imagination. Know that you're using your imagination powerfully, vividly, with strong intent to create the highest good.

I now ask and set the intention that any information that has been shared here with you brings you Peace, **Love**, Light, or something better. Take a deep, healing breath.

As you're tapping, you may also want to work with beautiful rose quartz or your favorite crystal. Crystals are our friends, and the crystals are fascinating. It is my understanding that there are Divas in the crystals. These Divas are not stuck in the crystal. They move in and out as they please. Let's visualize or get a piece of Rose Quartz, the Love Stone, and hold it. If you're a man, you might want a pocket stone. If you're a woman, you might wish to a rock a bracelet or favorite piece of jewelry. A man might even want to acquire a pendant. Whatever is comfortable for you. Ask that everything that has just transpired here, the Archangel Raphael Energy, the Archangel Camael Energy, the Archangel Sandalphon energy, the Archangel Jophiel energy, the Archangel Gabriel energy, the Archangel Orion energy, the Archangel Haniel energy, the Archangel Metatron energy, the Archangel Michael energy, the Archangel Raziel energy, the Archangel Uriel energy, the Archangel Zadkiel Energy, the Glowing Sun Angels, the Magnetic Moon Angels, the Violet Flame Energy, the blissful Dolphin energy, and the gorgeous Saint Martha energy **Be** infused with your Rose Quartz. Ask that all this energy, **Divine Love**, health, and Abundance infuse our Rose Quartz and ignite with crystalline magic. Crystals are generators that expand, so may all this **Be** expanded in exponential blessings for you and yours.

Let's take a deep, healing breath, and tap on the heart area. Deep, healing breath while you breathe slowly and let all this light infuse your body. Yes, very good.

"You are the powerful creator of your reality," as Abraham-Hicks says. You found this book at this time because you are ready to step into your power **Now**. You came to this earth to Dream Big Dreams, have a big life, **Be** happy, and I call in Archangel Jophiel again, so there is no judgment as to what a great life is. This is whatever you choose it to **Be**. Please do not compare your life to another, as this is counterproductive. I will give you this tidbit. If it makes you happy and is for the highest good, then that is what you came here to do. And you can find more of this with your Archangels, Tapping and your Breath-work.

This is the Archangel Breath-Tap, may it bring you great blessings, **Love**, Happiness, Peace, and Good Fortune. May you **focus** your mind for your highest good. May the Archangels, Saints and Dolphin Guides help you with this or something higher.

May you remember that feeling good emotionally is so valuable and worth every effort and may the Archangelology Series of Books and Audios help you with this.

I send you Peace and Blessings. May we all be blessed in light and Love. So mote it be, and so it is.

Thank you. Kim.

4

EFT GUIDE FROM ACTIVATE YOUR ABUNDANCE

Here is an exert from the book *Activate Your Abundance* also available from Together Publishing by Kim Caldwell. Here we get more detailed about the EFT tapping process for extended study.

AN INVALUABLE TOOL: EMOTIONAL FREEDOM TECHNIQUE (EFT)

Please be aware that back when I wrote this, tapping was not as prevalent as it is now. I included this for you, keep in mind that the simple tapping I presented at the beginning of this book is just as powerful. This section is not necessary, yet may enhance your process, so I included it for you. If it feels confusing in any way, then it is not essential to include it. On the other hand, you may love the more strategically placed tapping points. As I always express in all of my books, you know what is best for you and are the boss. Please enjoy the process.

***

"Most of our emotional and physical problems are caused (or contributed to) by our unresolved specific events, the vast majority of which can be easily handled by EFT."

---Gary Craig

The most important skill we can develop is the ability to identify and release unwelcome thoughts and emotions from our mind and body. Once we understand that our thoughts and beliefs are creating our reality, it is common to become afraid of our negative thoughts. EFT, also known as tapping, is the perfect enhancement to any program that encourages positive thought because it creates vast spaces in the mind for new uplifting thought to enter. EFT is a simple and effective tool discovered by Gary Craig that releases unwanted thoughts and emotions in order to reclaim untold peace. The priceless information presented here is also inspired by Natalie Hill, an experienced EFT practitioner.

EFT works with specific energy meridians we have throughout our body. We may tap on these points while holding an unpleasant thought with the **intention** of releasing this negative thought. Dr. Bradley Nelson, author of *The Emotion Code*, states, **"Intention is a powerful form of thought-energy. It is possible to release trapped emotions using the power of your intention alone. I believe that the intention to release the trapped emotion is really the most important part of the equation."**

The negative programs, thoughts and beliefs we hold actually start to drain our energy and create physical problems. Most people carry around these negative emotions for years without being aware that they are contributing to many of the problems and diseases they are experiencing today. It is to our benefit to clear out these self-defeating thoughts, much like clearing the clutter from our home. When we practice tapping we will start to feel lighter and happier. As a result, Divine ideas will start to come and delight us.

The intelligent practice of tapping is related to the science of acupuncture that dates back 2500 years. When we become conscious that we are holding a thought that feels uncomfortable, we can start tapping on the energy points and get relief. It feels like the tension just releases and we can think clearly again. For me it feels like an actual sigh of relief. The anger, depression, fear or even unwanted physical symptoms will simply become less prevalent. Be patient and keep at it. We may even find ourselves laughing as these thoughts lift and we feel relief.

Here is how to tap away your negative emotions and thoughts. Always use the tips of your fingers as they have their own energy meridians. This gives us double benefits. We may tap with our left or right hand; choose the one most comfortable, knowing you may switch hands when needed.

We want to clear on negative beliefs that keep popping up like, "I never have enough money," "I am not good enough," or "I need to lose weight." Of course you have your own personal negative beliefs you want to clear. Understand this: the act of clearing out these self-defeating beliefs is one of the most empowering practices we can do. Without these negative thoughts running rampant in our minds, we will start attracting the life we truly desire.

We may also tap on physical pains such as a stomachache or headache. There is a connection between the stomachache (and any unwanted condition) and the worrying. We start by tapping on our karate chop point (shown picture 1) and saying, "Even though I have this headache, I still love and accept myself." Now, listen for any thoughts that come up like, "Wow, this job feels like too much for one person to handle," and tap on that. We simply want to listen for what comes up and tap on it. The great thing about tapping is we are allowed to complain and vent out these negative emotions with the intention of clearing them out for good and feeling better. Our complaining actually serves a purpose when combined with tapping.

Let's do a round of tapping here. Let's tap on the common issue of feeling anxious. Of course, you may substitute any fear or negative thought you are dealing with and want to clear. Try this:

Picture 1 Karate Chop Point

Picture taken by Rachel Caldwell

1. Start by tapping on the side of your hand (see Figure 1) and say the setup statement, "Even though I feel anxious, I still love and accept myself." Say this set up statement 3 times. Keep tapping on your hand as you say your setup statement.

2. Now, move to your face meridians (all face meridians are shown on Figure 2). On the rest of these points we will just say a reminder phrase once

Picture 1   Karate Chop Point

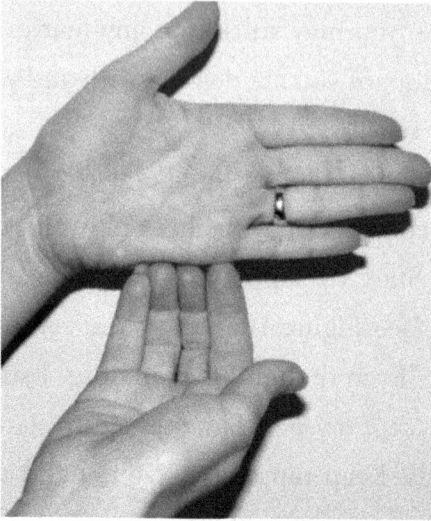

Picture taken by Rachel Caldwell

and move to the next point. The reminder phrase keeps you focused on the issue so tapping on these points can get the energy moving and allow healing and change. The first meridian we tap on is the eyebrow point. Tap on this area while saying, "This anxious feeling." **The more you can feel the negative emotion while tapping the more**

effective the release will be. When you go into the deep negative feeling of the stress while tapping, this is helping to release it for good.

3. Now, move to the side of your eye and tap. As you tap on this spot, continue to say the negative thought or condition, "This anxiety is making me cranky." Be open to any thoughts that come up and tap on them. For example, if the feeling, "I am tired of people criticizing me," comes up, tap while you say it.

4. Now tap on the spot under the eye and say, "This nervousness feels like it will never go away."

5. Now tap on the spot under the nose and continue to vent, "This anxiety scares me and makes me feel helpless."

6. Now tap on the chin where the diagram shows and say, "This feeling like I will never

get everything done, this nervousness in my body."

7. Now tap on your collarbone while making another statement that comes up like, "I hate feeling so anxious."

8. Now tap all over the top of your head with the tip of all your fingers and make another statement, "I am tired of this tension in my body that feels like it will never go away."

You have completed one round of tapping; it should go relatively quickly. Take a deep breath and just sit with yourself for a minute. Now it is time to evaluate. How do you feel? Has the unwanted emotion or feeling calmed down? If not, you may do another round of tapping until you feel the relief.

Once you feel relief, it is time to do a round of, "Wouldn't it be nice if...?" Be sure you feel ready before you start this round. If the tapping has not given you relief yet, continue to tap on the problem or take a break. If we try to move to our "Wouldn't it be nice if...?" round before we are ready, the mind will create arguments. When we do our "Wouldn't it be nice if...?" round, it should feel good like, "Yes, everything is feeling a lot better now." Take your time. Tapping may feel foreign to you at first.

In this round we put the question, "Wouldn't it be nice if...?" in front of desired statements. This allows our minds to accept these statements easier. Start tapping on your energy points shown below and make statements like, "Wouldn't it be nice if I could relax more often?" or "Wouldn't it be nice if I could go with the flow and enjoy my days more?" or "Wouldn't it be nice if I remembered my ability to attract the perfect people to help me?" Keep tapping on your energy meridians while you make these statements.

Once you feel good making your "Wouldn't it be nice if...?" statements, it is time to move right into your definite statements about what you do want with joy and knowing, like positive affirmations. Here are a few examples: "Everything is going to be alright," "I am managing my time better every day," and "I am going to get all the help I need." Now, we are commanding and back in our power.

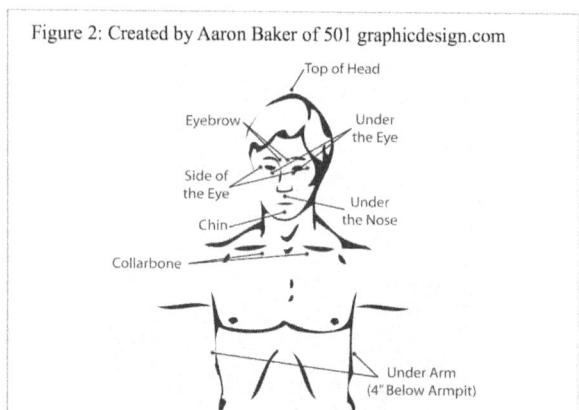

Figure 2: Created by Aaron Baker of 501 graphicdesign.com

Tapping is like anything else -- the more we do it, the better we will understand how we are responding and how much we need to practice. We get better the longer we practice. If you are having trouble believing that something so silly and simple could work, you will want to tap on that. For example, while tapping say, "Even though this is silly and will never work, I still love and accept myself."

If you find yourself in public experiencing negative emotion, there is a discreet way to tap. Natalie Hill explains that right when we feel the stressful emotion is the time to tap it out. If we are somewhere it is inappropriate to tap on our face, we may use the finger tapping technique just as effectively instead. Simply tap the right side of the nail on your pointer finger with your thumb. Tap your thumb and finger together about 10 times while saying the negative thought to yourself that is bothering you. Then, tap the side of each other finger with your thumb, just like you did your pointer finger. This way you may clear negative emotions anywhere, anytime.

Natalie Hill suggests that we make a written list of anything that has ever bothered us. Try to come up with as many as possible; at least 100 are a good start. Each day, tap on three of these issues. This cultivates a feeling of peace in our lives. Give this tapping technique a try and expect miracles.

5

ANGELIC MANIFESTATION
JOURNAL BONUS

C reate more of the life you want with the Archangels as you explore and focus with your Angelic Journal. If you are ready, let's set intentions now to make your Archangel Breath-Tap Book a Manifestation tool. It is said that humans have so many thoughts going on in our heads at once that it is hard for Angels and Spirit Guides to hear what we want help with. This is one of the many reasons it is so powerful to get very clear on what we desire and write it out in a designated journal for our Archangels. This way, they can understand our needs better and help us with our dreams and goals in Divine Time.

It has been proven that when we write things down, more of what we desire comes to us. Goals get accomplished, and things flow with more ease. Adding the Amazing Archangels to your journaling just makes the results that much stronger. As we set intentions for what we want and take the time to focus and write it down in our journal, unseen forces move on our behalf. We are going to enlist the help of this Divine Knowing with our Archangel book in an interactive way and turn our book into a manifestation tool. We are also going to play with our books like children and have some fun. Children are powerful creators, and we will take on some of their great habits for their creative value.

Focus and underline ideas you resonate with in your book and become immersed in Upliftment. There is a deeper connection as we become interactive with our Archangel books. We may get colored pens and underline areas of our book that feel important or special to us. We may want to draw pictures of desired blessings or anything that makes us feel good. We may want to mark different areas of our book with hearts, stars, or Angel wings. Get sticky tab notes, a personal favorite, and stick them to your favorite pages you want to return to often. In your journal section, place a sticky tab on an area you want to let the Angels know to help you write in and as a personal reminder. Let your Angelic interaction and intuition guide you with what feels best. Neville Goddard and Albert Einstein both explained that our imagination is a creative force and can bring great blessings to our lives. We will bring our imagination fully into our process now. You may want to add stickers to enhance pages. Place a beautiful angel or magic looking card in your book as a bookmark. Get creative and give your book some personal character. Putting clover or flowers in your book to press and dry, adds some powerful nature magic to your process. Roses are a great choice as they have the highest vibration of any flower. You may give lovely flowers as an offering to your Archangels as well. Giving back is always a beneficial activity.

Everyone has magical abilities. Some of us know this, and some do not. My point is all these ideas are simple and will work for anyone who puts forth an effort and has the faith to relax and let go so the angels may do their work. Of course, anything we put out comes back to us, so we want to always include "for the highest good" in all requests.

In all my studies of magical herbs, cinnamon is found in many different traditions for enhancement of all things wanted and removing things not wanted. You may want to rub a dab of cinnamon mixed with a touch of olive oil on your journal in an intentional shape such as a heart for more love or the infinity symbol for more abundance. Then say to yourself, "I anoint my journal with success and happiness with the help of the Archangels." Anointment has been practiced for eons with much luck and advancement. Basil and Sage could just as easily be utilized. Anything that feels magical and speaks to you in your spice cabinet most likely has wonderful magical properties. Use these gifts of nature with intention and focus for a more joyous life. The idea is to create a magnet for all you desire that is for your highest good with your Archangel Journal.

You may want to underline ideas in colors that mean something to you. The sky is the limit, get creative and juicy with your book, knowing that amazing things are being created.

Next, we have dedicated pages that are waiting for you to fill them with your heart's desires that the Archangels, your Dolphin Guides and St. Martha will help you achieve as long as they are for the highest good. You may write anything you want in your Archangel Journal. There is no right or wrong way to do this. You may ask the Archangels to help you release things from your life, share your hopes and dreams, or ask questions. I ask my angels questions, patiently wait, and know they will lead me to the answer in Divine Time.

Be open and honest with your journaling and the Archangels understanding that the only ones who need to see your Angel Journal are you and your Angels. Keeping your wishes to yourself is very powerful for manifesting as well.

We have created categories for you, and of course, there will Be freestyle areas, so play with this and have fun. After you play with your journal, you may put it away in a sacred space knowing all is in Divine Order. Remember, magic works just in its own time and asking where the results are will only block things, so relax, have faith, and patience. Keep this powerful journal; you will be pleasantly surprised when you check on it at later dates. You may come back to read your Breath-Tap book and add more to it at any time. Know that unseen beneficial forces are moving to help you now and forevermore. Play with and collect other Archangelology books and audios, remembering, "If you call them, they will come." Check out the Archangelology Archangel Journaling Book for more ideas on taking your Journaling Process to the next "celestial" level. The Archangels have tied this whole series Together for us in such a Divinely Intelligent way. Spend time in nature with your book, filling it with **Love**, imagination, and Angelic Magic for exponential results. You are a powerful creator and loved by all that is.

Write on the blank areas of your book

and on the lined journal areas. Think outside of the box and let your kid like creative energies flow. Have fun, and add your own flair.

Please enjoy the process and expect wonderful things.

6
___

BREATH-TAP JOURNALING

W rite out some of the things you would like to accomplish with your Breath-Tap at this time. Your focus will evolve. Come back and Update this when inspired.

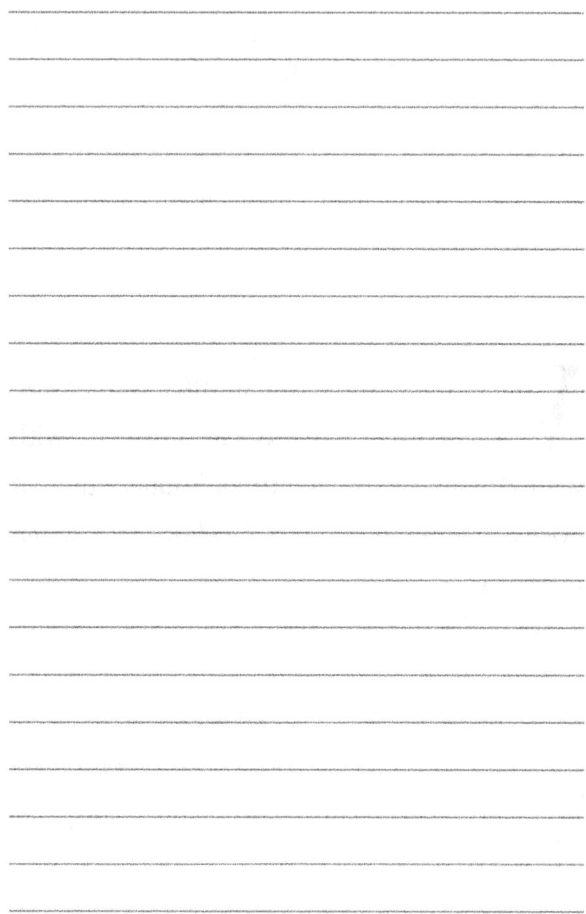

I AM CREATING NEW THOUGHT

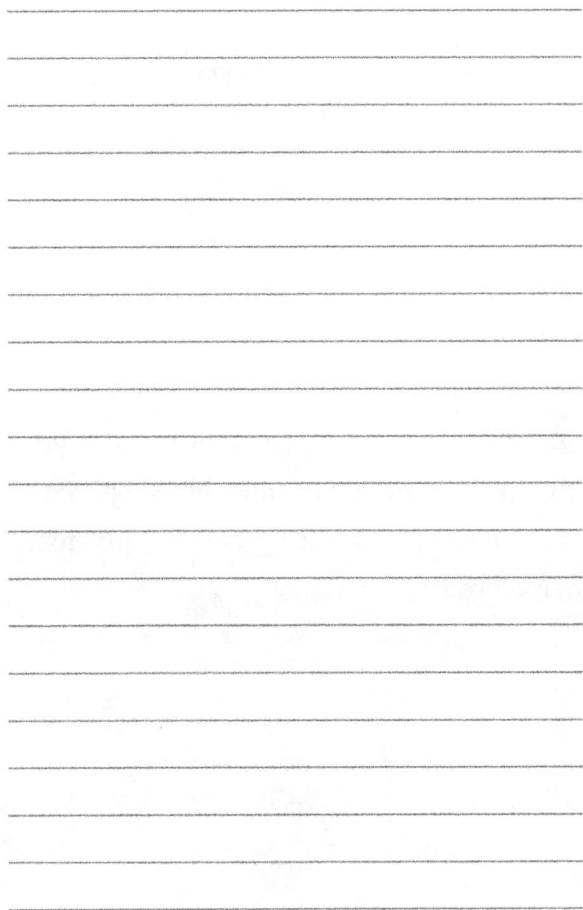

7

LIGHT ANGEL BREATH TICKLES
MY NOSE

I Am getting more conscious of my breath. Write out times you want to work your breath for more peace and blessings. Write out times you notice your breath focus helped you.

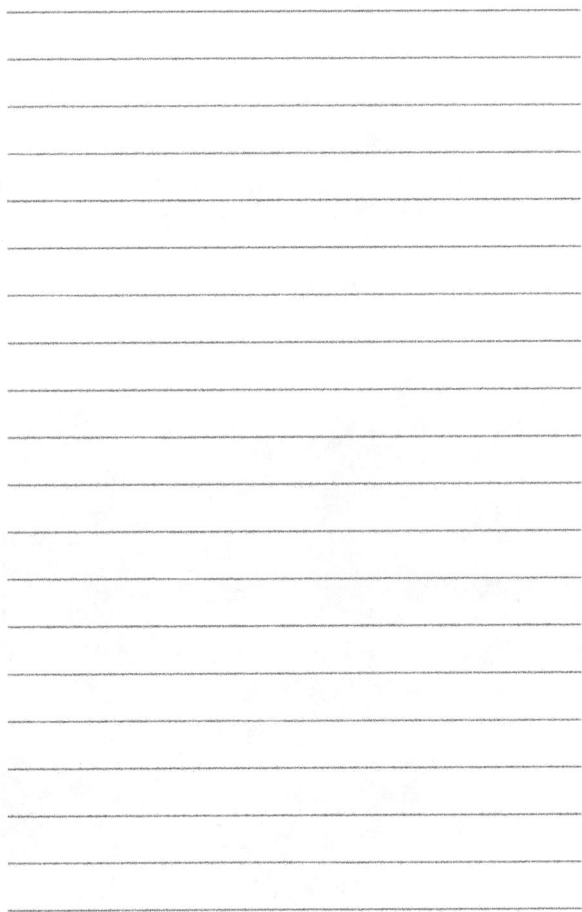

I FOCUS WITH THE HELP OF MY
ARCHANGELS

J ournal about the things you want to Focus on creating more of.

8

FINANCIAL BLESSINGS JOURNALING

My financial goals are accomplished with the help of the Archangels.

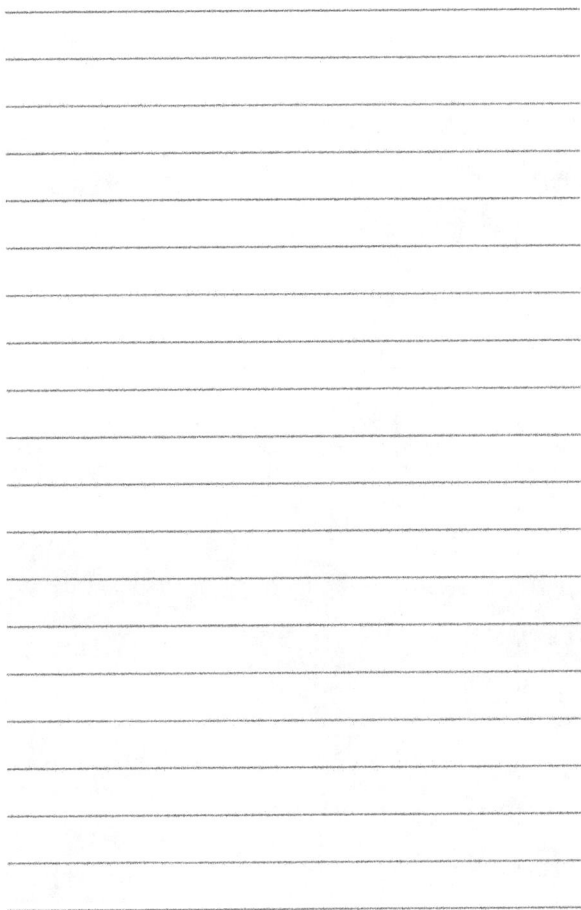

I AM ABUNDANTLY BLESSED
FOREVER FREE GLOWING
GOD/DESS

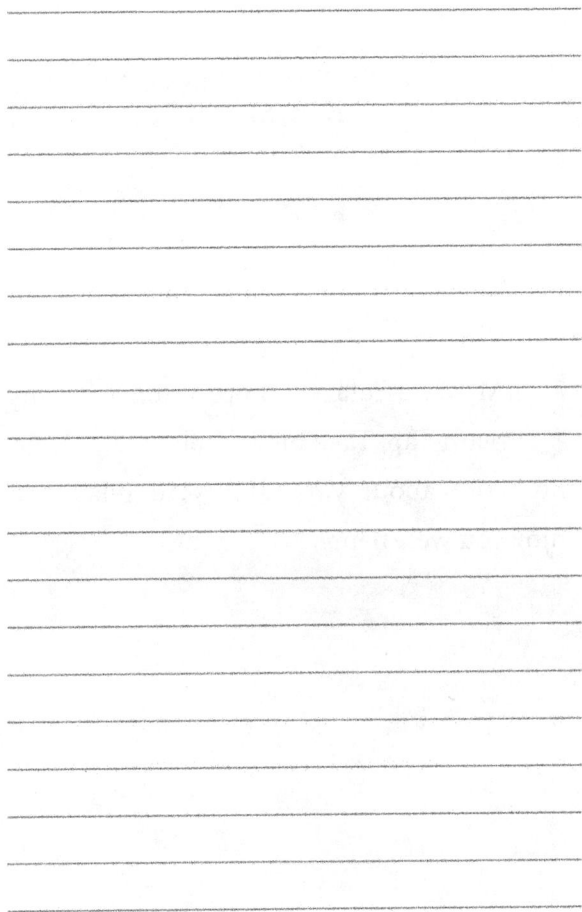

9

I FLOAT IN THE AIR LIKE AN ANGEL

I AM more relaxed more often with my Breath-Tap. Take more time to daydream and write about your ability to relax and enjoy you well-being.

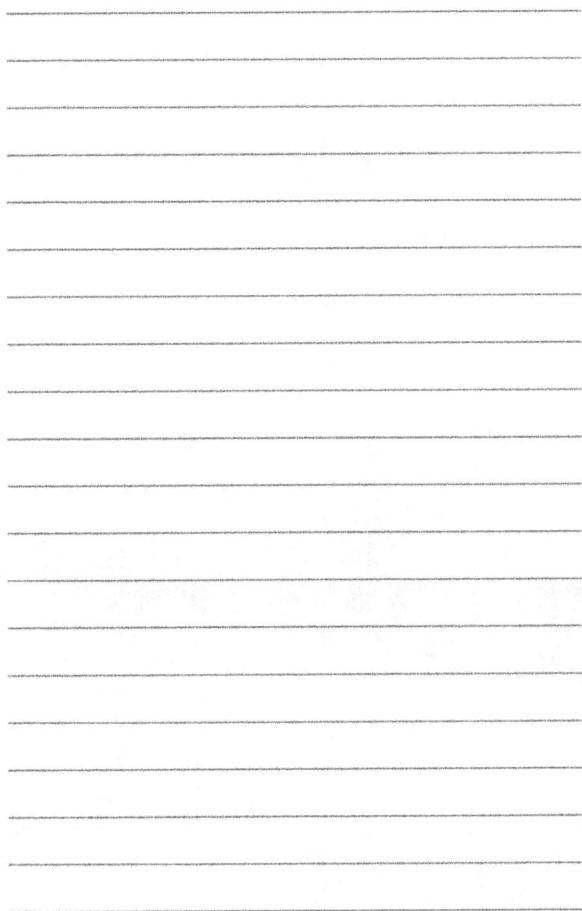

I AM LAUGHING AND
HAVING FUN

MY WRITING IS FILLED WITH ANGELS

I take deep breaths and the words just flow with Angelic Messages into my Journal.

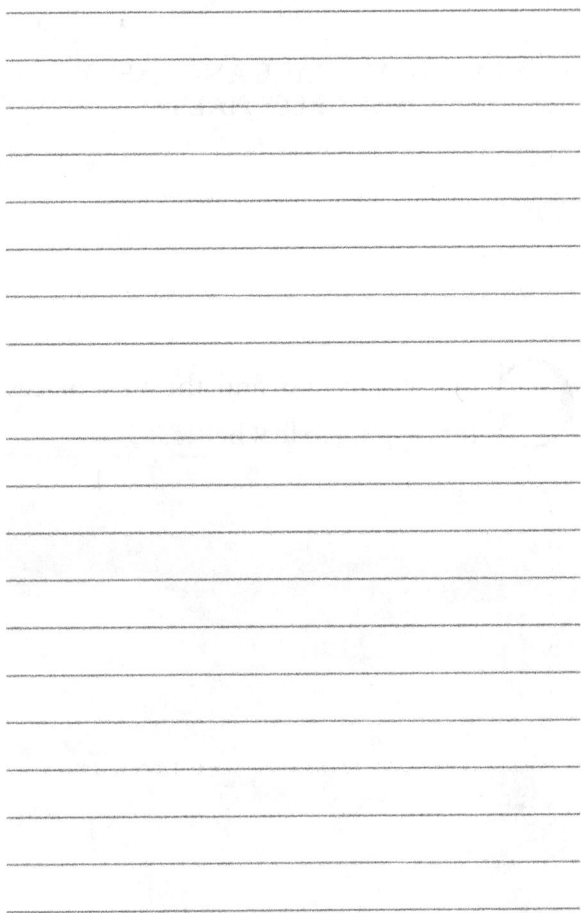

10

I TAP WITH GRACE AND EASE IN
THE CELESTIALS

G et creative and find the best places for tapping to feel better.

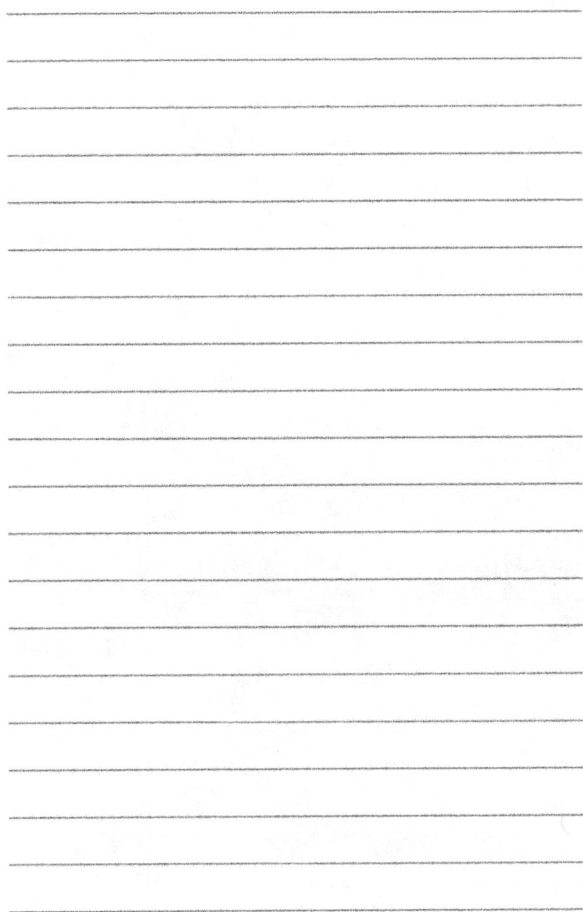

**SOMETHING MAGNIFICENT IS
HAPPENING.**

I Take Deep Healing Breath and feel how
Abundant and Blessed I Am.

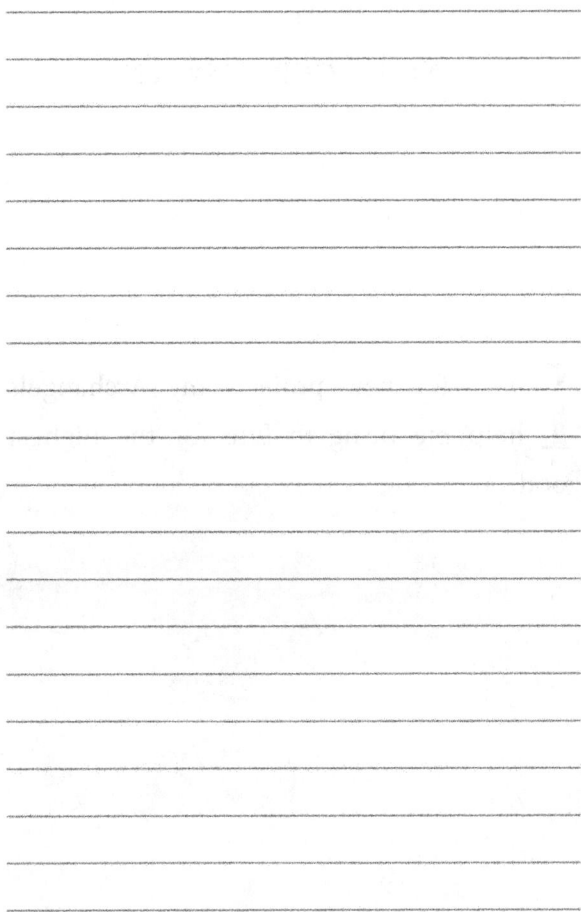

11

ANGELS GUIDE MY PEN

Ideas for new projects my Archangels help me bring to Life for the highest good.

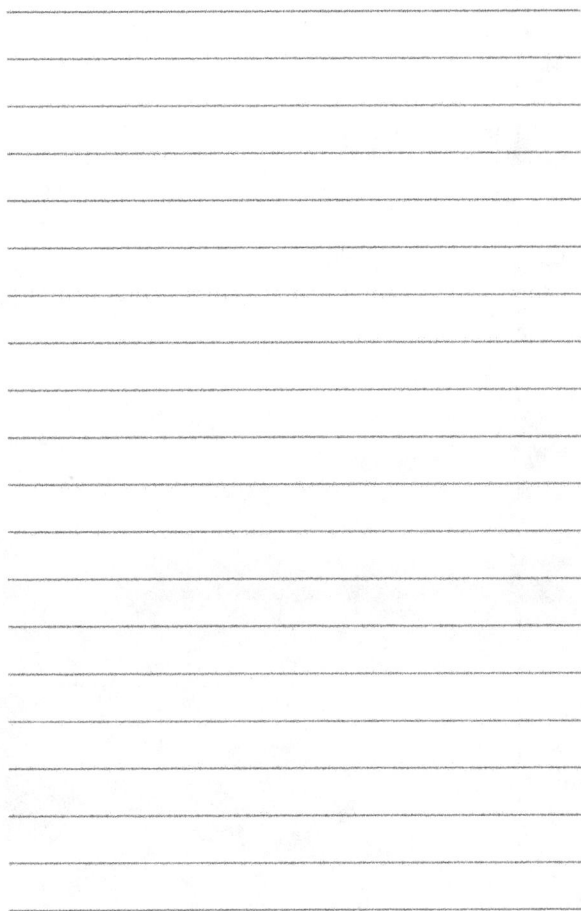

BREATH-TAP TIME TRAVEL

Now that you have found Breath-Tap think back to a time in your life when you wish you had this knowledge and could have used it for your benefit. There are those who believe we can change our reality by working on our past. Release those emotions now and journal about it.

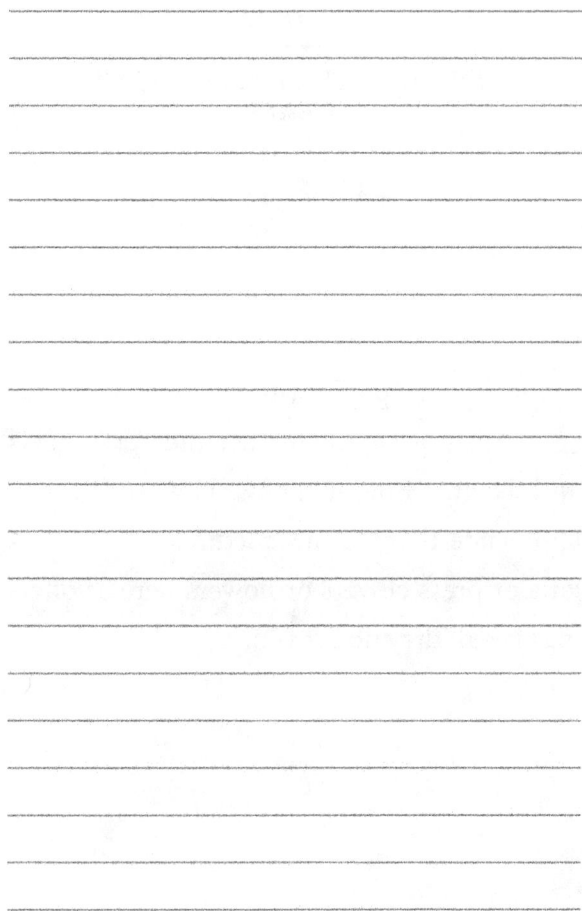

12

DEEP GRATITUDE FLOWS ONTO
MY PAPER

Fill these pages with the things you are truly grateful for. Let the Archangels and Divine Energy know how much you appreciate them. Draw pictures for them as gifts or press clovers or flowers here as offerings for all they do for you.

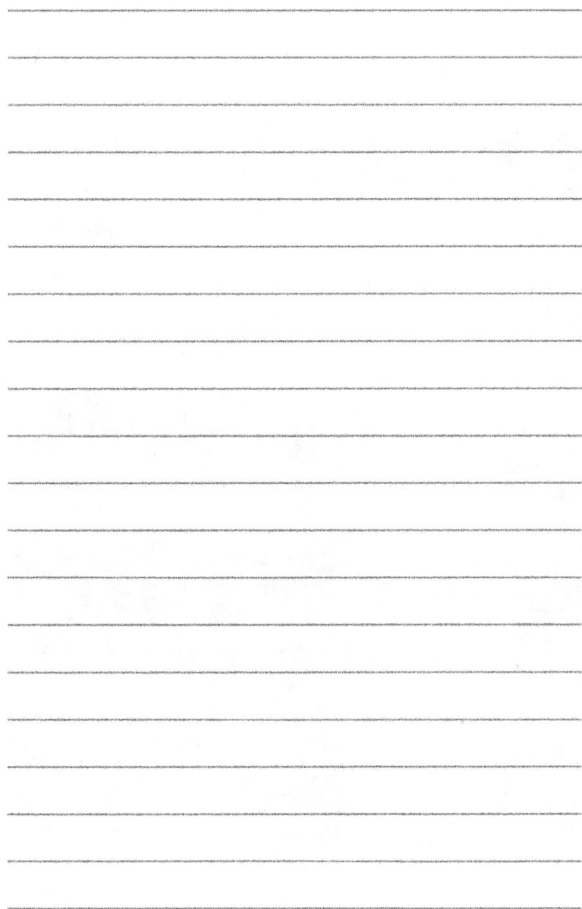

SET 10 SACRED MINUTES A DAY TO COUNT YOUR BREATH

S it with a timer set for just 10 minutes in complete quiet listening to your breath. After you are done, if inspired, Journal all the lovely things that come to you. This is a magical process, and with consistency, expect a more wonderful life.

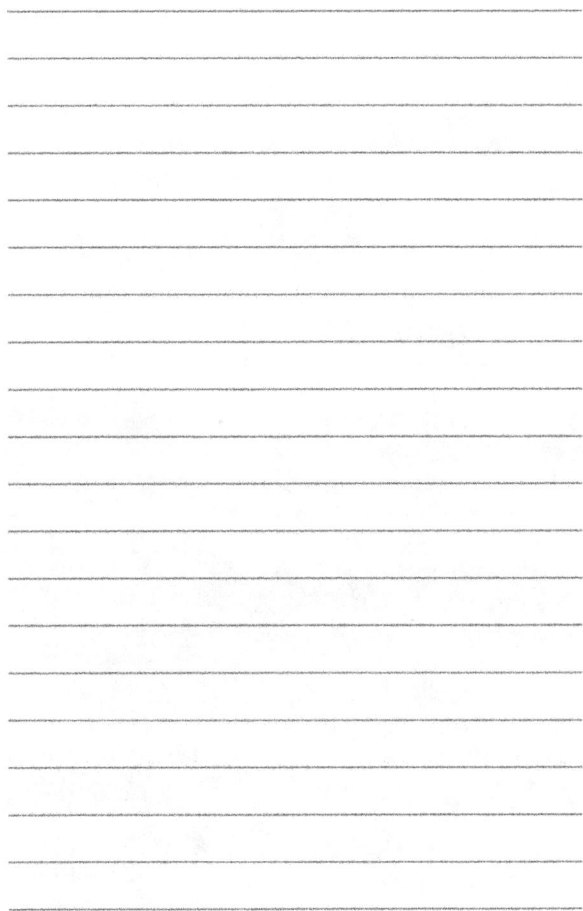

I SMILE AS I TAP BLESSINGS INTO MY BODY.

Write out some positive statements that you are going to tap into your body for a positive self-image. Examples are I am Enough. I am finding more things to Love about my life.

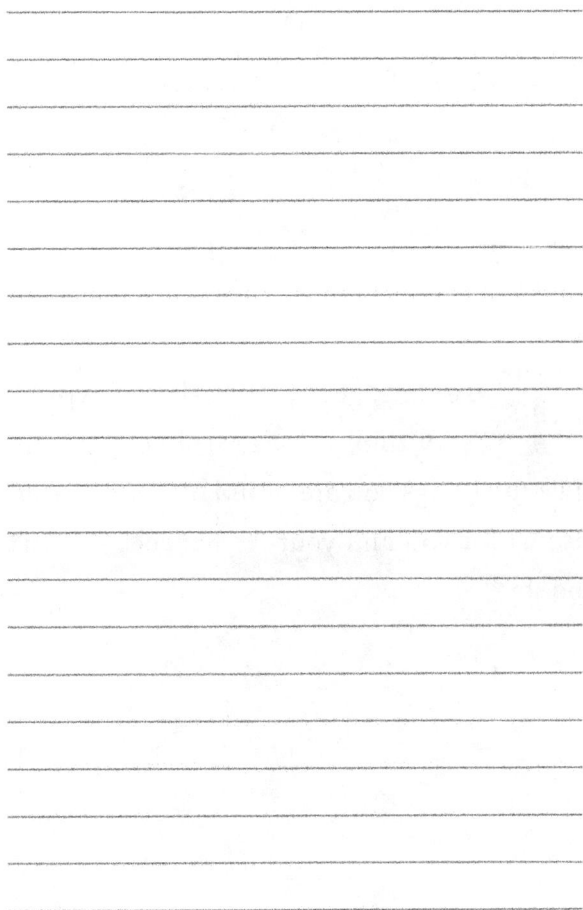

13

I TAP LOVE INTO MY HEART

Take time, get by yourself, and write a list of things you love about yourself. List the things you are proud of. Your journal is just for you and your Archangels, so don't be shy.

14

BLESSINGS

~

May the Divine Creative Force that Moves and Creates the Universes Bless and Enhance Every Wish You Ever Conceived that is for the Highest Good of All Involved. May Joy, Peace, and Purpose Be Yours all the Days of your Lives. Through All Time Space and Dimensions. So Mote it Be, and So It Is. I hope this book helps you in wonderful ways and radiates out to a gorgeous future for you and yours.

Kim

REFERENCES

Amora Quan Yinn. The Plediadian Workbook. Awakening Your Divine Ka. (Bear & Company 1996).

Anna Merkaba. Mission To Earth: A Light workers guide to self mastery. (Merkaba Healing Inc.).

Catherine Ponder. The Dynamic Laws of Healing. (DeVorss Publications).

Christopher Macklin. Dissolving the Enigma

of Divine Healing. (Christopher Macklin Ministries Inc.).

Chaudhary Sufian. World of Archangels: How to Meet an Archangel. (Sufian Chaudhary 2012).

Damon Brand. The 72 Angels of Magick. (Damon Brand).

Esther and Jerry Hicks. The Essential Law of Attraction Collection. (Hay House).

Florence Scovel Shinn, Your Word is Your Wand. (Compass Circle).

Inna Segal. The Secret Language of Your Body. (Simon Schuster, Inc.).

James Mangan. The Secret of Perfect Living. (James Mangan)

John Kreiter. The Magnum Opus. (John Kreiter).

Kyle Gray. Angel Prayers, Oracle Cards. (Kyle Gray 2014).

Matias Flury. Downloads From The Nine: Awaken As You Read. (Matias Flury 2014).

Og Mandino. The God Memorandum. (Frederick Fell; 1st edition (1980).

15

MORE OFFERINGS

~

Visit http://www.togetherpublishing.com to discover more Archangels and Super Power Saints

Each of the following books has a matching audio filled with healing music.

Archangelology Michael * Protection

Archangelology Raphael * Abundance

Archangelology Camael * Courage

Archangelology Gabriel * Hope

Archangelology Metatron * Well Being

Archangelology Uriel * Peace

Archangelology Haniel * Love

Archangelology Raziel * Wisdom

Archangelology Zadkiel * Forgiveness

Archangelology Jophiel * Glow

Archangelology Violet Flame * Oneness

Archangelology Sun Angels * Power

Archangelology Moon Angels *
Magnetism

Archangelology Sandalphon *
Harmony

Archangelology Orion * Expansion

~

The items below come in book only

Archangelology * Archangel Journaling

Archangelology * Archangel
Breath-Tap Book

How Green Smoothies Saved My
Life Book

~

Activate Your Abundance Book and Audio
Program

~

The rest of the items below are available in Audio Format

Archangelology * Breath-Tap Super Power Saints Volume 1 Audio

Archangelology * Breath-Tap Super Power Saints Volume 2 Audio

Regeneration Meditations * Switchword Series with Solfeggio Frequencies audio

Radiating Divine Love * Switchword Series with Solfeggio Frequencies audio

Love Charm * Switchword Series with Solfeggio Frequencies audio

Dragon Sun Grounding Meditations * Cosmic Consciousness Series audios

Sweet Moon Sleep Meditation * Cosmic Consciousness Series

Enchanted Earth Sacred Geometry * Cosmic Consciousness Series audios

SUPER POWER SAINTS BREATH-
TAP AUDIOS

M

eet the Super Power Saints

Available   now   at

https://togetherpublishing.com

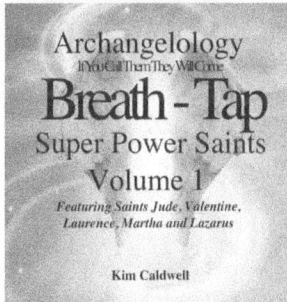

Archangelology
If You Call Them They Will Come
Breath - Tap
Super Power Saints
Volume 1
*Featuring Saints Jude, Valentine,
Laurence, Martha and Lazarus*

Kim Caldwell

BE AN ANGEL

I f you enjoyed this book or received any help from it please give it a positive review so others may find it as well. Thank you so much for your time.

Kim

www.ingramcontent.com/pod-product-compliance
Lightning Source LLC
Chambersburg PA
CBHW060354090426
42734CB00011B/2131